CRASH *AND OTHER POEMS*

CRASH

AND OTHER POEMS

by

Louis Gallo

Adelaide Books
New York / Lisbon
2020

CRASH: AND OTHER POEMS
a collection of poems by
Louis Gallo

Copyright © 2020 by Louis Gallo
Cover design: Adelaide Books LLC

Published by Adelaide Books, New York / Lisbon
adelaidebooks.org

Editor-in-Chief
Stevan V. Nikolic

All rights reserved. No part of this book may be reproduced in any manner whatsoever without written permission from the author except in the case of brief quotations embodied in critical articles and reviews.

For any information, please address Adelaide Books
at info@adelaidebooks.org
or write to:
Adelaide Books LLC
244 Fifth Ave. Suite D27
New York, NY, 10001

ISBN: 978-1-952570-29-2

Printed in the United States of America

Contents

CRASH: A SEQUENCE OF VARIATIONS   9
IMPACT   11
BLOOD ON THE AIRBAG   12
APPLE SAUCE   13
YOUR HAND   14
REINDEER   15
AMULET   16
AHAB   17
WITHDRAWAL   18
WHEN YOU'RE NOT HERE   19
IT IS I   20
THAT FORMAL FEELING AFTER GREAT PAIN   21
LEAF   22
SWING SET   23
WHITE HUMMINGBIRD   24
THUS CONSCIENCE DOES MAKE COWARDS OF US ALL   25
FACETS   26
WHAT WOULD YOU SAY   27
TOMORROW   28

ZERO/INFINITY   *29*

MOTHER OPENS THE FAMILY ALBUM   *32*

IRONY   *37*

BURNING   *39*

"I BARELY ESCAPED WITH MY LIFE"   *41*

ON THE WALK   *44*

TAO   *46*

UNDERTAKER'S DAUGHTER   *47*

UNIVERSITY POOL   *48*

DREAM RECIPE   *50*

JONATHAN EDWARDS   *52*

BUGSY   *53*

THE EXISTENTIALIST   *55*

SEVEN AND A HALF WAYS TO RUIN A POEM   *56*

BLACK BOX   *58*

LA BELLE DAME SANS MERCI   *60*

CAPITALISM   *63*

GOLDFINCH   *64*

BRASS TACKS   *65*

EMY'S PATIO, Bourbon Street   *66*

NARCISSUS   *68*

INFORMATION THEORY   *70*

GUESTS   *72*

D.H. HOLMES DEPARTMENT STORE CLOCK   80

THE STREETS OF THE VIEUX CARRE   82

NEVER START OR END A STORY WITH A DREAM   87

LEGS   89

CROW   92

CLEANING LADY   93

ALL I WANNA IS NORMAL!   95

ER   96

WITTGENSTEIN: A BIOGRAPHY   97

SECRETS   99

THE QUEEN IS DEAD, LONG LIVE THE QUEEN   100

"A LOOSELY CONSTRUCTED THING"   101

Acknowledgments   105

About the Author   107

CRASH
A SEQUENCE OF VARIATIONS

IMPACT

> . . .nothing comes from nothing,
> The darkness from the darkness. Pain comes from the darkness
> And we call it wisdom. It is pain.

--Randall Jarrell, *90 North*

She tells me it's good that I can't remember but I want to remember, I want to peer into the eyes of the beast that almost killed me though I, Lazarus, have tentatively returned—

I yearn to confront the evil head on, which in a way I did since it knocked me out cold, a sudden nothingness, ex nihilo, only to awaken flat on my back in an ambulance hurtling in strafing rain out of Hillsville to Galax then the Trauma Ward at Wake Forest Baptist. They cut off my clothes with a scissors and knife, another degradation I can't recall. It's good, she insists, because I saw it all and believe me you're better off not seeing. I envy her. It's a kind of gnosis, an on-the-spot revelation. And I love her more because she did gaze into those eyes, because she grasps what I can only suffer after the fact, ignorantly, stupor of stupors, the bog of forgetting or never knowing or, or blind submission.

BLOOD ON THE AIRBAG

The purpose of literature is to turn blood into ink.
                    --T.S. Eliot

When Justin brought her to the service garage in the mountains where they had towed the mangled Rogue, the first thing she spotted was my blood, splattered and encrusted, like rust, all over the airbag. She admits she went berserk, pranced hysterical, maybe shrieked as she rushed about, encircling the vehicle, gathering what had survived, seeking answers to which there were no questions. I lay doped up in Trauma an hour away half keeping an eye on the invasion of the Keys by another monster, Irma. I mourned the Rogue in my way by not mourning it at all. The nurse asked if I'd like some chicken noodle soup and apple sauce. Sure, and yogurt too. Cathy and Justin transferred whatever they could into his truck. Her glasses had lost their lenses. Someone had stolen the GPS. The new ice chest and its cargo, vegetable soup which she had made especially for the girls down in Winston-Salem, was crushed, that soup, like my blood, anointing the ruins. I think chicken noodle was the first thing I tasted after my resurrection. Good, it tasted so fucking good. I even tried a soda cracker, which I never eat. Cathy's homemade vegetable was better but I could not drink it. No one would ever drink that batch, bloodied as it was.

APPLE SAUCE

The silver apples of the moon,
The golden apples of the sun.
    --Yeats, Song of the Wandering Aengus

The entire month of September, including my Virgo birthday on the Sixth, lost to catastrophe, mayhem, pain, opioids, confusion and forgetting. She tells me I was hooked, a cyborg, to constant beeping machines, including the usual heart rate and blood pressure measures; two IVs squirming out of each crook of the arms; a billion blood tests (all ok, except low on potassium once—so they wheeled in an aluminum scaffold from which hung a bolus of potassium solution); countless x-rays and scans—

all in all, 24 pages of medical test results faxed to my doctor in the Blue Ridge. Yet through it all I could eat—and indeed felt constantly hungry. She tells me I always ordered apple sauce, yogurt, French toast, sometimes a tuna sandwich, sometimes soup—drinks too, apple juice, orange juice, good ole h2o, ah, and coffee. I remember only the apple sauce, how perfect it seemed, that smooth texture, the slight tang, the easy slide down the throat, hints of cinnamon and clove. The perfect food for convalescence—
hell, I'm still devouring it weeks later. So why am I recalling the Greek apple of discord; the Biblical apple Eve couldn't resist; an apple of my eye somewhere buried in the deep past? The worm in that apple?

YOUR HAND

Love is the hastening gravitation of spirit towards spirit, and body towards body, in the joy of creation.
                              --D.H. Lawrence

They've nestled me away in this swanky room distant from the other patients because, from what I've glimpsed while making the rounds with my physical therapist (a sweet girl who chats incessantly about how to roll into and out of a bed rather than plop down into or rise precipitously from) everyone else here is, believe it or not, worse off than I am. They lie unconscious in a series of rooms off to the side of the nursing station
one,
a young man whose face is now a red, raw smear, the epidermis having been scraped off on asphalt; another who has lost a jaw—rods and wire now welding his skull together;
and most alarming, someone glazed in a total body cast with only a black vacuole of a mouth puckering back and forth like a ravaged, mutant jellyfish. What's a xylophone of broken ribs next to such defilement? How I feel for these fellow victims, how I long to assuage their ills with some hocus-pocusy flick of the wrist. How lucky I am to be holding your hand in this room as the evening darkens and transforms us into gentle shadows, your hand in mine.

REINDEER
What's madness but nobility of soul
At odds with circumstance?
      --Theodore Roethke, In a Dark Time

Each night as we lie together I clutch and stroke your fingers as if they pull me from a depth I detest more than fear. I prod you for more details, anything else about that week when I slid in and out of consciousness, three different narcotics seeping into my veins. I don't know why I crave knowing exactly what happened, nor do you, but I ask ceaseless questions, mostly the same questions, and you supply mostly the same answers; the repetition soothes me, lulls me, and begins to acquire a reality I feel directly, if only vicariously, a kind of osmosis.

You tell me that you dozed in the chair beside my bed every night, that the girls visited for long stretches every day, that Justin sat beside you holding my hand, that Eric raced down from the Blue Ridge to see me. I don't remember any of it but yearn to, to remember the memories as my own. Because all I have are tiny bits and pieces, a blurred pastiche. And every now a then you recall a new delicious detail—when you came back from the bathroom and I, wide-eyed and startled, informed you that a reindeer had bitten my elbow. Then I lapsed once more into cloud-cuckoo land, a pleasant enough place for the not quite dead.

AMULET

The world is full of magic things, patiently waiting for our senses to grow sharper
--W. B. Yeats

It was my daughter Claire who made sure I executed the deep breathing sessions upon every commercial break during normal tv programming—as instructed by the doctors. She also brought for me a goofy rubber crab I had once found in a Myrtle Beach gift shop and which she keeps on her bedside table. I held that crab tight in my hands and instantly understood love. On our most recent visit to Winston-Salem I spotted it again on one of her shelves and asked if I could have it. She shook her head and smiled—"No, Da, you gave it to me." This too I understood. How selfish of me to ask for any more magic than it had already bestowed.

AHAB

Reach me a gentian, give me a torch
let me guide myself with the blue, forked torch of this flower
down the darker and darker stairs, where blue is darkened on blueness.
--Lawrence, *Bavarian Gentians*

Long as I can complain I ain't dead, defunct or oblivionized. Don't think I complained once while lying semi-comatose in Trauma suffused with mind/body numbing drugs.

I'm not even complaining now, sort of. We were smashed by a massive 4X4 white Ram-like pickup truck. This I'm told because I don't remember the collision at all, knocked me out cold. But since the telling that white truck haunts me—I dream about it; I envision it heading for us again and again. Ahab's white whale. I am now Ahab, obsessed, no peg-leg but with wounded ribs and clavicle. No revenge to seek, no Pequod, only the desire to obliterate whiteness, that no-color containing all colors, that whirlpool dooming Poe's Arthur Gordon Pym.

White. Give me black, penumbra, opacity, the black lantern of D. H. Lawrence's Bavarian Gentians. White, too visible, merciless, non-descript—make mine dark, shadowy, noir, raw umber will do. My Rogue was charcoal. The white Ram consumed it, mangled it, sent it to the graveyard. No, in thunder. Don't call me Ishmael.

WITHDRAWAL

An unknown sphere, more real than I dream'd, more direct, darts awakening rays about me—So long!
            --Walt Whitman, *So Long*

They pump poison into your veins to lure away pain; otherwise you would surely writhe in anguish. When the pain abates they release you and supply the same poison in white pellets. You live for the pellets until they turn on you and induce their own new ache-protest against being hated and abandoned.

You find yourself stalking the empty halls, fidgeting, itching, delusional, exhausted—and you feel you're worse off than before though you don't remember before because poison had anaesthetized you. Four days, you're told, for it to flush out of your system, four days to return to humanity. And it's only day one. You figure you can't endure, that you'll swallow the entire bottle of white pellets and be done with it. But you don't, you endure and invent reasons to suffer—and to rejoice.

WHEN YOU'RE NOT HERE

Were I with thee
Wild nights should be Our luxury!
     --Emily Dickinson

When you're not here Furies and demons swarm from every crevice, from the shadows and woodwork-- even shafts of sunlight filtering from our curtains seem desolate and cold, when you're not here I become a phantom in my own house, a ransacked ghost, when you're not here my heart sprints in an empty arena, my corpuscles scream silently, when you're not here nothing seems vibrant or even alive when you're not here, I exist only residually by proxy, what's left over, nothing, when you're not here.

IT IS I

I can't go on. I'll go on.
            --Beckett, *Molloy*

It is I, I whisper to the walls that seem to recoil from touch as I pace and repace these familiar yet unfamiliar wooden floors, up and down the stairs, back and forth, sleepless, deranged, It is I, house, remember me, now revenant at these ungodly hours, the town asleep, the town silent, It is I, yes, undone but struggling back, muddled with drugs that numb pain but create new pain of their own—it is I.

Thought I wouldn't be back, eh? Nor did I. There is a vast chemical industry coursing through my blood, into my heart and brain, and while it is certainly I (who else could it be) it is not I—just as you can't go home again, though here you are, home again despite imperceptible differences you can't discern—same old pastel walls, pine floor planks, humming appliances—but rather feel. And they feel you as well, welcome you back cautiously, you could be an imposter, yes, certainly a subterfuge, for Lazarus did not return as Lazarus after all; disguise, guise, decoy. I flick on a light switch and the room floods darkness into another darkness, the kind you can see, the bright kind, and, look, a mirror! and it's you, I, gazing into another forest.

THAT FORMAL FEELING AFTER GREAT PAIN

I thought I was in hell;
therefore I was in hell.
             --Rimbaud

Emily nailed it on this one though I might add "during" as well as the inevitable "after"—
that gasp of revelation, no benign Sunday school, little Golden Book, Rockwell versions (though Norman's personal life was wretched) perhaps:
the sense of ablution after your first Holy Communion; or the transfiguration you witness as you stand before the mirror in your rented tuxedo hours before the prom;
what the Slavs call "litost," catching sight of yourself in a storefront window and panting in disbelief--new territory, you the wagon master heading into a canyon, or, say, when someone drives a flare into your chest and you stand dazed, stunned, incredulous as you sink to your knees knowing all along that you expected it—the casual formalized.

LEAF

> *The skies they were ashen and sober;*
> *The leaves they were crispéd and sere—*
> *The leaves they were withering and sere;*
>   --Edgar Allan Poe, *Ulalume*

I sat on my deck this morning prepared once again to bemoan my fate when a tiny Buddhist in the form of a curled, brown leaf from the silver maple cascaded down and adhered to my knee. To regret, said the Buddhist leaf, is to amplify. Just let go, flow, savor the moment.

I admired the little sage but laughed: the opioid has already achieved as much; I have no choice but to float in the ephemeral, though I have always relied upon choice in matters of body and soul. A gust swept through and whisked away the bodhisattva. I watched him twist, curl and bob with the wind. I swear there was a pirouette or two in the diaspora, dancing as the swan sings.
I lay back my head and laughed and the Bo Tree blossomed.

SWING SET

Marie, Marie, hold on tight.
    --Eliot, The Waste Land

Shortly after the damages inflicted by Katrina on my family down south and the psychic damages up here I paid Home Depot to erect a massive play and swing set in the back yard to sooth the girls. The play set has long since deteriorated but the swings still work just fine. For twelve years I sat on the deck and watched as the girls, iPods attached, arced back and forth to the squeaking hinges that no oil would soften. The goose-like noise itself became a comfort, and I felt content hearing it, knowing my daughters safe.
 But control is a false thicket. The girls have moved away, the swings abandoned. So here I sit once again on the deck, this time with my own internal Katrina of broken ribs. I try to ignore the empty swings. In truth, the girls had outgrown them but out of habit, and their own comforts, they would mount and sway to their music. The yard is still, silent, strange—dead leaves spiral from the trees. From the corner of my eye I glean movement—and, look! the swings have suddenly started to sway of their own accord. There is no wind.

WHITE HUMMINGBIRD

I can imagine, in some otherworld
Primeval-dumb, far back
In that most awful stillness, that gasped and hummed,
Humming-birds raced down the avenues.
                              --D.H. Lawrence

I.

Maddie told me the other day that as she sat on the balcony of her second-story apartment a white hummingbird hovered in front of her eyes for a few seconds then zipped away. I want to see it too, that rare hue in hummingbirds, right before my eyes—for a long time. It left a single feather on one of the pine boughs. She could not reach it.

II.

THUS CONSCIENCE DOES MAKE
COWARDS OF US ALL

When I allow myself to brood upon the collision I try but cannot remember I become either apocalyptically numb or envision confrontation by tanks in a terminal global conflict—smoky cordite fumes blind us, the discharge of pervasive artillery deafens us, and we scramble into trenches sodden with mustard gas.

Or I alchemize the horror into the feather of a rare white hummingbird shed upon a pine bough beside my daughters' apartment, the feather I've finally reached over and hold between my fingers, a most sacred gift, the hummingbird, my mother tells me, an omen of choice of her and my father, decades ago, before I was born, before I had ever seen such a bird, before everything.

By "conscience" the Prince meant "consciousness" (which Dostoevsky or Freud or one of them described as a disease) that grave mistake of evolution, that serpent in the thicket, interloper and despoiler. Brush it away with a white feather.

FACETS

What has been is what will be,
and what has been done is what will be done,
and there is nothing new under the sun.
　　　　　　　　　　--Ecclesiastes

To clear the air of the Preacher and that dour wretch Baudelaire I turned to Looney Tunes and Dancing with the Stars. I might as well have been on Mars. Reality is no Key Lime pie though devour it we do. It does not pay to rue our days as if suffused in the daze of regret. What we get we get, the sweet madeleine cakes that transported Proust, the bitter herbs of Christ. They are the same in kind to those who aren't blind.
Life is life and death, death, they say, as if devoid of common sense and breath. Look between the lines, beneath the bottom, above the top:
something stupendous is going on. Why grieve what's gone or to come? Focus on the eye blink of the sun. What is has not yet begun.

WHAT WOULD YOU SAY

Alien they seemed to be;
  No mortal eye could see
The intimate welding of their later history. . .
  --Thomas Hardy, *Convergence of the Twain*

. . . what if I told you that I had foreseen the crash long before it actually happened, decades ago, when I was a child? You would not believe. I have passed years as a watcher of omens and signs and portents—I've seen the shadows, the basilisks and dragons, those mystic informants. They hang in space, a deep basso throb before discerning ears evolved, until they piloted Attila to Rome, the Titanic to the iceberg, the Fuhrer to Berlin, and the white whale toward Ahab's leg and my ribs, toward you too. We call this destiny. We call this Fate. Evil. Naming clarifies chaos, palliates mayhem. No distinctions before names. Feeble distinctions after names, names that enable us to proceed as if we're behind the steering wheel. Wittgenstein: the bewitching of intelligence by language.

TOMORROW

> *. . . tomorrow and tomorrow and tomorrow*
> --Shakespeare
> *Yesterday came suddenly*
> --Paul McCartney

Some days mope along, tortoises, but their reptilian cumulative effect is to break the sound barrier, a rent and crack in the ears of your heart, a blatant beast, this airy substance we call time, though not a substance but rather the purveyor of substance, a metaphysical medium of sorts, what we can't buy at CVS or Walmart but would love to at any price because it's fickle and peremptory as that girl I tried to woo back in high school, the one who always disappeared around a corner before I got a good look or could speak.

Mystics call it an illusion as well as some physicists who point out that it is reversible in quantum equations. What a lie! When I passed my last birthday flat on my back in the Trauma Ward I might have believed, opioided . . . but no, it's no illusion. Look into the mirror. Remember Nineveh and Carthage and the great empire of the Hittites. Whither? All tortoises in their day. Which day? Tomorrow. It came before yesterday, before your birthday, before itself, before time. Can't make your peace, can't . . . not with an explosion. We are the illusions of history, the sleights-of-hand, voo-doo will-'o'-the wisps.

ZERO/INFINITY

Zero and infinity always looked suspiciously alike.
                              – Charles Seife

. . . il faut s'abêtir
                              – Pascal

I suck at math, still count on my fingers, uno, deux, drei . .
but the discipline nevertheless, like Sirens, allures me
even if I'll never grasp how certain minds can (grasp)
demons like square roots, calculus, pi, imaginary numbers
(imaginary? hallucinations? how possible?)
but indeed they do and often lose their lives or sanity
in pursuit. . . the entire Pythagorean school slaughtered
by enemies, Pythagoras himself slain as he fled
because he refused to cross a bean field en route
(he hated beans); Zeno tortured and hacked to death
while biting off the ear of the tyrant of Elea;
Archimedes stabbed by a Roman soldier –
he didn't move when so ordered because he was busy
trying to solve a math problem . . . and I guess this poem
is really sort of a book review of *Zero: The History
of a Dangerous Idea* that I found in Good Will, by a guy
whose dust jacket photo makes him look twenty-five or so,
a kid, but a kid who's on to the wiles of zero and infinity,
those not so rare birds that make me cringe –
and I should really be fixing that leak in the bedroom ceiling
or the one upstairs or a third from the kitchen faucet
(leaks everywhere! . . . like Gödel's Theorem:

every closed system is really open, leaking into greater
closed systems, which in turn are really open, ad infinitum –
sounds like Aquinas looking for God, eh?)
rather than wasting time with ideas dangling permanently
beyond me, Tantalus straining for the apple or kumquat,
but I get enamored, hooked by their sinful attar
and sultry swollen lips and mini-skirts and spandex . . .
and it seems the Occident rejected both zero and infinity
for nearly two millennia because of Aristotle
who despised and feared voids that threatened
his neat, orderly, Windex-glossy plenum,
a tidy, rational universe, no holes or leaks,
whereas the Babylonian zero (naturally Babylon –
the idea just HAD to originate in hell)
was received as a friendly guest by first India
then China for it complied with their notions
of Atman, Brahma and all that, whereas
we Greeks and Romans luxuriated in Aristotle's dream . . .
and now in the book we're up to the greatest mathematician
of all time, Georg Cantor, who proved impeccably
that zero and infinity often disguise themselves as each other
and moreover there are an infinite number of infinities, some
larger or smaller than others (my mind has shut down now,
I just read the words, yearn for my wrench and plumber's putty)
and Cantor went miserably insane, spending the last years
of his life in an asylum beset by infinite Furies and that ghoul Zero,
but finally, with Cantor, we Greco-Romans
realized that you need Furies and ghouls to, what?
invent calculus, which spawns relativity and quanta . . .
though new problems arose because those damned infinities
kept ruining the equations, the ultraviolet catastrophe,

& on and on and on . . . so they "re-normalized" the math
and dumped the infinities once again (isn't that cheating?)
and looks like, now that we know so much, the universe
will expand forever and meet its heat death a few trillion years
from now (no phantasmagoric Big Crunch, no return to a singularity,
another zero that, get this, occupies no space, the entire cosmos
occupying no space) . . . what the? . . . I turn to my repairs
with joy and relief, tighten the wrench around the nozzle,
exert a bit of force, loosen the cap, pry out the eroded washer,
replace it with a brand new one from Lowe's, retrace my steps,
turn on the faucet and, feeling strangely anointed,
pour myself a perfect glass of water
that is both half-full and half-empty.

MOTHER OPENS THE FAMILY ALBUM

Here's a great-grandfather,
nobody knows which.
See the bullet lodged in his forehead?
Lived with it forty years
protruding like that,
imagine.
People were different then.
When it fell out
he stuck in another one
carved from bamboo.
Little Richie.
When he died
Uncle Ambrose shrunk
into a raisin so black
they had to buy more lamps.
Aunt Lil says he slept
with Richie's picture in his hand.
Now that's love.
Such a nice little boy too,
gentle as mist.
There's evil out there
and it's hungry.
That's what gobbled Richie up.
Remember Miss Cleezio?
Don't give me that, sure you do.
She scared you to death.

When she came over, in the kitchen . . .
remember? She laughed so hard
she peed all over the linoleum.
We like to died.
Don't tell me you don't remember
Miss Cleezio.
This is blind Hankie
who lived next door with Mary
and Miss Yundt.
Why'd you hate Miss Yundt so much?
God, she must have been
a hundred years old even then.
He gave you bright new pennies
and you let him run his fingers
across your face.
He played piano
in a Bourbon Street night club.
See, no matter how unlucky you are . . .
God, the zinc salve they smeared
on his skin for acne.
That's why he smelled so bad.
You adored Hankie
(oh, yes you did)
but he made Ruthie nervous.
I guess he's dead now, like everybody.
Look, it's me!
Wasn't I gorgeous?
About fourteen, maybe,
when I first met your father
on a bus.
I swear he followed me

all the way to Canal Street
and back.
I was bringing MaMaw's watch
to Adler's for cleaning.
If he doesn't just plop down
on the seat and start talking
a mile a minute.
I was so flabbergasted
I didn't say a word the whole trip.
Then he found out I lived
around the corner.
Well, you know what happened.
I told him I was eighteen.
Two weeks later he proposed!
I never once looked at another man,
before or after,
and don't think I didn't have the chance.
It's Tony, that black fellow
who worked for your father
down at the shop.
Never a peep out of him,
always showed up on time,
you can't find a man
like him today.
Then he went berserk
in one of those places they go
and started stabbing people
with a screwdriver.
Don't you know
one of the drunks walks up,
points a pistol at his forehead

and pulls the trigger.
Daddy heard it was terrible—
Tony's head split right in half
like a coconut.
Uncle Jake, what a nasty old man.
They put him away after Emma died
until he got caught in bed
with a nurse!
He only had one tooth
and no mind at all.
What's wrong with people?
She was half his age
with three children.
One of them died of polio.
Well, they kicked Jake
out and fired her.
He went back to the house
where he and Emma used to live
and just sits there in the dark.
For years now.
If it wasn't for a neighbor
who kind of looks out for him . . .
Not me, I wouldn't go there
if you paid me. That man
always had roaming hands
even when Emma was alive.
Used to corner me at the parties.
His fingers felt like tongues.
Honey, I'm glad you're here
but I can't keep my eyes open—
oh look, you and Ruthie

at the beach, this was Florida,
Tarpon Springs, I think,
remember the wonderful sponges!--
we can look more tomorrow
if you want. I'm falling asleep.
Memories make you tired.
When I think how I used to keep going
hour after hour . . . day and night too . .
nothing good about getting old.
And look at you! And Ruthie,
I'm worried about her.
How'd so much happen to us all?
In so few pages.

. . . oh, look—this is really old.
I think they call it a tintype.
We don't know where it came from.
Doesn't it look like a skull?
So corroded you can hardly
make out anything.
I've tried to wipe it off
but some grime just doesn't clean.
You just live with it.

IRONY

I just read that gravity is not a force driving you down
As you slouch in your rocker, brooding, but the rocker's power
Pushing you up. Now, does that make sense? Einstein, natch.
So how deal with speculations that defy everything we know,
Let's face it, we could not have dreamed up gravity
If our mother's lives depended on it . . . no, thank another genius
For that, Newton, an utterly paranoid man who saw angels.

Because we everyday lifers don't need gravity–though some levity
Wouldn't hurt–we don't need quanta and protons and dark matter
(now they're telling us that ninety-six percent of the universe
Is missing!) and ultraviolet catastrophes and double slits
That "prove" light is both a wave and a particle at once.

Almost like saying you can be dead and alive at once,
Like that famous cat. No, we can do without metaphysics and
Theoretical physics and Dr. Phil and anything that makes us
Fear and distrust our own minds. When I clutch a brick I don't
Want to know that it's composed almost entirely of empty space–
Tiny atomic solar systems, all that vacancy.
(And now we hear that electrons are not sub-atomic
Children going round and round on a carousel–they're smears
Shrouding the nucleus like mist, like phantoms.)

Louis Gallo

I want a solid, redolent, meaty brick, a macho brick,
And I want to spread equally sturdy mortar on one side
And affix it to another brick and I want to build a wall of bricks
That withstands hurricanes and tsunamis and any genius
Who comes along to inform me that my brick wall
Is an illusion, get lost! We must shun education altogether
And get back to carriage bolts and cedar shingles and 2x4's
And concrete slabs and maybe a glass of Merlot or two.

Grapes, now we're talking. And don't tell me how Merlot
Is made. I don't want to know. Or how to build bridges
That will collapse. Or why chickens cross the road.
Down with what we can't see, taste, feel, hear and smell,
Though if something's got to go, take smell. I've inhaled
Enough foulness for a lifetime and so have you.
Henceforth we shall staple our faith onto the real,
Not the imaginary, not the far out, not weirdness . . .
Faith in thumbtacks, charcoal, each other's flesh, chicken soup
(those who didn't make it across), rocks, salt tang of the ocean.

And, of course, faith in King God basking in heaven as He suffers
Our every mewling prayer, bestows manna and mercy,
Redeems the miasmal, contagious ignorance
Shrouding our cores, our own nuclei, with His breath.

BURNING

This inches toward the beginning, the dripping moss of dream, myth, delight . . . riding with my father and sister in a primed pick-up, its bed loaded with sawdust-packed cardboard drums, our trek to the vast dump on the outskirts of New Orleans, a place long since buried under housing developments. I am five and my sister nearly two years younger; she doesn't remember much so I improvise for her as the truck coughs, stalls sometimes, lurches along a narrow asphalt road between profuse curtains of oleander, crepe myrtle, banana trees, clacking bamboo stalks, lush red berries Dad warns us not to eat. Poison, he says.

The trip takes forever, but always, sooner than we expect, we fork onto a mud path where Dad gets out to open a rusted wire gate with its smudged "No Trespassing" dangling from one bent nail. A flat, smoldering wasteland that stretches to the horizon: mounds of trash and debris, battered shells of automobiles, yellowed refrigerator doors frozen open like sad old tongues, cracked pipes, sofas split in half, tables, one-legged chairs, broken bottles, naked and lonely windows, mattresses with springs coiling out like solidified voltage . . . nothing worth having, though once I found a Duncan yo-yo good as new except for the bubbled, charred side.

My sister and I poke around with sticks as Dad unloads the drums—sawdust clouding like powder into his face. It's best in the little winter we have on this edge of the continent; then we bundle into heavy flannel coats and wear mittens. The fires feel good. Fire . . . the whole place is on fire . . . scalding and so dangerous you have to watch where you walk to save your shoes, your feet. The mounds of trash flare at will.

We scoot among them and hope to find a spot that won't erupt. Everything black and sooty, smelling like tar, the sky red and obscene. Glowing embers streak through the air like wild flaming insects. And here my sister and I romp, Dad's eye on us every second. You wouldn't take children to such a place today, you'd be punished, for what else can you call it but hell?

But we think it's cool, weird, good scary, secret, like the places in nightmares, somewhere beyond earth, an adult horror to glimpse before being whisked home. Don't think I'm striving for accuracy, an equally mythic playground— no, we amputate the past as we spiral down its still point zero. The bits and pieces might even fit differently in another puzzle. Could be the place occupied no more than a city block and the only fire is the one Dad kindles to burn sawdust; the entire trip might take ten minutes, not hours. No bamboo or banana trees either, maybe only the usual dull bushes along any road. Red poisonous berries, though, that's a fact – say the only fact, the sole remaining icon and atom of what was everything. Life just seems better when you lather it with legend and memory, those Windexed mirrors of your long, clean life that begins in a lousy dump that glows and hisses like the very dust and gases of the universe at the beginning, not the end, of time.

"I BARELY ESCAPED WITH MY LIFE"

The lacquered reporters declare another miracle
as we now deem the merest rosy swerve from doom
a glittering token of divine twitch.
Minicams pan the charred fuselage
with highly resolved devotion,
zoom slowly upon a shadowy figure
who emerges from the sizzling wreckage.
I barely escaped with my life, she exclaims,
the lone survivor, a Civics teacher,
early forties, dazed, someone you won't recognize,
always one of us, already losing the battle,
though she clings to her plaid overnight bag
and looks intact enough but for patches
of sooty rouge baked into her cheeks.

But who is this I who escaped and with whose life?
Is "I" separate from the metabolic stew of hormones,
enzymes, corpuscles, protoplasm and pulsing jellies?
Suppose she had barely escaped without her life —
returned to Bradley High in the swank part of town,
its antiseptic brick and quicksilver windows,
computers in every class, perfumed kids
with names like Misty and Sean, driving
Volvos and swollen with the yeast of good luck.
You know their elegant uptown mothers
who can't give up leotards or Merit ultra-lights,
an hour at the spa before cruising the coffee shops
for lavender tea and heavenly cream puffs,

the boutiques and Langenstein's,
a sternly Caucasian grocery with exotic delicacies
like chocolated ants and rum bon bons
exquisitely priced to make one feel perfect.
So troubled their lives, what with Misty pregnant
and Sean howling as he shoots spiders in the attic . . .
who could begrudge the Prozac, the martinis?
Lives worth escaping or heaven on earth —
that is, the best it gets in this hive?
Their children, languid clouds of resentment,
file into school corridors that reek
of puke, Tampax and leathery old sweat.
Moon-faced, they stare at the wonder
who stands before them with new assignments —
Mrs. Xnitious? — on the civics of the soul,
the cartography of beatitude
and ecclesiastics of the bardo.
Will it be on the test? they want to know
before it's back to scratching emery boards
and blasting Aerosmith into gray matter
that took a million years to evolve.
Mrs. Xnitious — we know her too now —
drifts from desk to desk with the glow
of a bodhisattva shorn of flesh and desire.
She is everywhere, here in room 202,
in Yukon forests she has always longed to visit,
hovering at the rim of the known universe
beyond which lies a sea of pure radiance.
She has side-stepped time and place, suckles
at the breast, slouched in study hall with *Cosmo*
hidden under homework, stands at the altar

as Mr. Xnitious slumps over a steering wheel
ten years later, feels the plane begin to vibrate
and rip to shreds before it crashes,
staggers out again to meet ravenous reporters,

I barely escaped with my life

wears the face of each student from birth to death,
howls with Sean, lies with Misty on a cold stainless gurney
as blood and a ghostly infant crawl down her thigh,
squeezes into a leotard and giggles over tea and brioche,
feels Mr. Xnitious penetrate, his breath labored,
sweat dripping into her eyes until that final shudder,
strokes his cheek in the open casket, no longer merely wife
but mother as well and daughter, unsteady on her feet,
on their feet, the feet of all who have barely escaped
with our solitary, grievous, sundered, beautiful lives.

Louis Gallo

ON THE WALK

On the walking trail I encountered
a mother coming toward me,
she pushing a stroller with a new babe
and a rambunctious tyke hopping
beside her, hooting, singing, leaping
everywhere.
He rushed up to me as we approached
each other and declared, "I was born
in 2010!'
I looked him in the eye, smiled, and replied,
"So was I!"
The tyke's face went concave, his eyes
bulged, his jaw dropped. "You were?"
Oh, the fiendish taken by surprise.
I wanted to explain to him that every day
is our birthday, that each day we rise anew,
that each night we die and each day
is therefore also our deathday,
that in a thousand years, maybe a hundred
none of this will matter and we'll all
be forgotten . . .
but no, I spared the tyke, no point
to the dire.
"Just kidding," I said, "I was born
ten thousand years ago."
The tyke frowned. The mother now

upon us shook her head with annoyance.
She was beautiful, trim, and looked fierce
enough to pounce.
"Cute boy," I said in passing, and the baby
too." I think under her breath she hissed,
"Asshole." And I longed to explain
that each of us has a different definition
of asshole, that one man's asshole
is another man's cerebral cortex.
But, no, I just walked on, whistling
a dirge by Faure.

Louis Gallo

TAO

The mounds and ridges of snow have not melted.
How odd they seem now, Styrofoam props
that no longer blanket these mountains in silent ease.
The cat mews at our front door--no food,
I guess. Earlier the sickled sliver of moon
rose only inches about the street. I thought
I would drive right into it and pressed the gas.
Skunks out back rip open plastic garbage bags,
feast upon remnants of lasagna and pop-tarts.
My little girls sleep daintily like moths upstairs.
In another room the television flickers
with static between stations.
I must add water to the cast iron pot
atop the wood stove.
We wake with caked blood in our nostrils.
A creak in the joists reminds me to call Richard
who will shake his head and say, "Not good."
The secret universe devours our house
floating in space like a candle.
Sirens hum in the distance; a voice in the street,
"Fucking whore, I'll kill you!"
The phone has rung all day. We don't answer.
The only mail is a pizza brochure.
One of our gutter pipes has come detached.
The basement floods, but I've sealed the roof.
There are birthdays to remember, supplies to secure.
A silver spoon falls to the kitchen floor tiles
and splits in two. Our amaryllis blasts its red
throughout the rooms. I hear dust settling.
The years stampede wild in every direction
like rice flung at a wedding.
I mind each nuance, whir and ping.
Lao Tzu rides out of history again on an ass.

UNDERTAKER'S DAUGHTER

You scooped jacks
beneath a marble bier
as your father parted the hair
of the beautiful dead.

Mary, the light was bad.
This was not untimely death.
Your father's lonely zeal
 robbed you of its splendor.

It was a living, God knows,
until he too was taken under
and you counted the stitches
in his cracked blue lips.

UNIVERSITY POOL

Two foreign girls in bikinis
chatter wiry Slavic as they sprawl
in lawn chairs facing the sun,
mysteries, reciting poetry perhaps
though I make out "K-Mart" among
the rolled r's, thwicks and ka-ka-ta's.
They leaf through Victoria's Secret catalogs,
sigh, throw back their bounteous hair.
The blond looks about eighteen,
here now, in of all places, a cul-de-sac
of the Blue Ridge mountains.
I imagine her village in Slovenia
or some black-and-white decimated place,
austere, desolate, blasted with history.
She lugs a pail of water into the hut.
Grandfather, flat on his straw mat,
groans and blisters with sweat.
Spiders crawl out of his mouth.
She swabs him down, sings old songs
and dreams about a television show,
Baywatch, where everyone is beautiful,
modern, cool and permissibly naked.
She will come to America, get in on,
learn the ridiculous language.
They stuff the old ones away in America.
And it's ok to expose enough breast,

buttock, abdomen and thigh to assure
that no one ample enough will ever
carry another water jug on her head
or shiver on straw again.
In America she will lie in the sun
as it gushes like butter into a bowl
surrounded by mountains that look like home.
The brunette, of course, is another story.

DREAM RECIPE

Here's a recipe I dreamed the other night,
which may say more about the quality
of my dreams than the dish itself –
slice the top cap off a green pepper, gut it,
line the insides with baby Swiss cheese,
fill the hollow with hummus (the kind
with artichoke and spinach bits),
Progresso bread crumbs, diced tomato
according to taste, a sprinkling of capers,
a teaspoon of minced roasted garlic,
garnish the top with sprigs of Italian parsley
and celery seed and herbs of choice . . .
now, would you eat this?
Sounds rather appetizing,
so I will, someday, when I find time
to gather and mix up the concoction.
But it's the dream that haunts me.
What has the unconscious come to:
piddling recipes one might find
in *Good Housekeeping*?
Don't think I'll call or e-mail Daniel
for an interpretation. Or Freud
who would no doubt declare
the hollow a womb, and the stuffing . . .
Now Daniel's dream of four malign
beasts rising out of the sea,

especially the ten-horned monster,
now we're talking, Daniel
out-Nebuchadnezzaring Nebuchadnezzar!
MENE, TEKEL, PARSIN . . .
such scribbling on the wall.
But who needs another apocalypse?
Think I'll stick with the recipe;
Think I may just have every ingredient
stored in the cupboards and refrigerator,
all save the pepper, the vessel.

JONATHAN EDWARDS

There, mumbling in circles, "infinite upon infinite,"
the gaunt, hunched, profoundly disturbed shadow,
tallying up his sins, so formidable, he deserves
to be stowed *below hell*. So he skulks
into the howling wilderness, harnesses his horse,
awaits, sweaty, apprehensive, waits for Jesus
to ravish him again and again, delights when the sword
pierces him, dust caked upon his lips,
his clothes ripped, his flesh mutilated.
He returns to the chapel and terrifies
the congregation: *you dangle in that web,*
angry Spider God inching closer,
hungry to devour you.
America's greatest, most erudite theologian.
No one reads his tedious stuff anymore.
He's reduced to a poem and a narrative—
or rather, segments of a narrative
in The Norton Anthology.
Count the number of times he uses the word "sweet"
when recounting his defilement.
He dies after convincing the congregation
that inoculations are safe. They aren't.
Below hell now, fathomless, he preaches on,
eternally, to demons, shadows, whorls of blackness,
a gathering condemned to listen
to his infinitely sweet tirades as Satan
slobbers over him, whispering "my darling,
my darling, my life and my bride."

BUGSY

Never quite right they always said,
that dog scratches himself
more than he breathes, more fleas
on that dog than mosquitoes on Louie—

>Louie, that was me, mosquito magnet
>on sweltering summer evenings
>before they sprayed the swamps
>with white cumulus gas that smelled
>like sugared evil

I remember a hectic blur,
salami-speckled, writhing in dust
to crush the swarms
assailing him like tiny Visigoths,
his short, spiked fur no relief

But he had a good personality
        the kind of dog that would crack jokes
if he could, impersonate John Wayne or Bogey,
slip a whoopee cushion under your rump
Disgusting, sure, but fun
        so I guess we loved him

When he started to bash his head
against the towering wooden fence
separating back yards then
we feared the whole thing might collapse

I see now
the flare of my mother's powder blue skirt
as she slides out the kitchen door
to lift all four of us kids
atop the roof of a little lean-to
my father had tacked onto the shed,
tar-paper sizzling with froth
under a sun churning heat like butter

      The alarm in her voice disturbs us—
Ruthie is still in diapers

We huddle atop that oven-of-a-roof
in spasms of panic,
the gritty surface scalding our skin
I manage
a peek at Bugsy, who—as we will celebrate
in story after story—rams his skull
into the fence with methodical passion,
a lather of foam burgeoning
from his lips and snout

Distemper, they would whisper, the word
      floating into my mind like a feather

And I remember a tear from me,
      Louie, the sentimental one
who knew mosquitoes, demons,
what they can drive you to,
even clowns like Bugsy

THE EXISTENTIALIST

I stood where I like to stand on the brink,
a mere twitch from the center, an eye blink
from the fuss and commotion, the merriment,
because I prefer to straddle an edge
where one can dredge from the cornucopia
broken wish bones, twisted curlicues of woe,
the shadows and detritus of history
any wind blows beyond the sight of those
who don't want to know what lurks behind
carnival masks of sorrow and joy
which cauterize the mind against outrage.
So I've cast out guises, turned the page,
not because I want to know but rather
to ascertain what dooms or saves us,
to gather the scrolls as we flit from one
square dance to another, learn how to weather
what storms beset us, howling tempests
we neither expected nor entreated,
inflicted at the outset, for no reason,
the pangs of birth, the treason of death.
Better instead to don straw hat,
click heels and whirl about the stage
with padlocked eyes, crushing the rat
whose incisor brain chews illusion flat.

Louis Gallo

SEVEN AND A HALF WAYS TO RUIN A POEM

1

Poetry is the supreme affliction,
Madame, the hum of those
who spin on spinning stones.

2

Poetry is the supreme addiction.
Sinking fast, we eye the ballast.
When no trinket shimmers in the mind,
we chink knickknacks from the soul,
that soft load.

3

Poetry is the supreme restriction.
We would ride the express-
ion beyond its rails
and bask in clear atomic broth,
wordless.

4

Poetry is the supreme prediction:
euphoric before-sayings, promises
broiled in poignant sauce.

5
Poetry is the supreme rendition,
a supple diminution
and false return:
lipstick and rouge
on the ape's blue tongue.

6
Poetry is the supreme exhibition.
Let those who frolic in pastures
strip themselves of berries
and frantic tendrils.

7
Poetry is the supreme friction.
Your hunger, Madame,
magnetizing
coiled silence and creamy coos.

71/2
Poetry is the supreme malediction,
Mater, Madame, Muse,
beware, beware,
flashing eyes and floating hair--
short end of the fuse.

BLACK BOX

Each morning, driving my kids to school,
I pass this shack on the corner where an old man
slouches blissfully asleep in a battered porch chair,
a porch chair *now* anyway, though once no doubt
the pride of his living room. Its stuffing oozes
from rips and holes in the arm rests. The upholstery
has faded to the color of bleached onion skin.

The kids cry, "It's the old man again!
He must be a hundred." They think hundred
because of his long, untrimmed, mossy beard
that bushes out in every direction. Asleep,
always asleep beside the piles of junk crammed
beside him on both sides, he, a drowsy guardian
of worthless lamp shades, TVs, push mowers.
The objects are indistinct, some tarped diligently,
some secured with rope, others sagging with age,
weight and exhaustion. It is not without surprise
that one day we find him standing amid the clutter,
stooped, indistinct as his possessions, the beard
now pinned behind his shoulders as he examines
a black box clutched in his hands.

And that's about all you can say –
a dusty, chipped black box about the size
of an old wooden camera, though not a camera.
A black box – cardboard or probably metal.
And he's staring intently into it as if startled.
We pass, the girls giggle, "That old man's
not dead after all!" and drive on to school.

After they're delivered I re-retrace my route
and pass the house again. He's still staring
at the box, grinning as he yawns, a caricature
of pleasure. I am reminded of the black box
of physics, the diffusion of gases and ultimately,
an ultraviolet catastrophe, all of which adds up
to a breakdown of natural law, reason, reality.
I'm tempted to stop, rush to the porch
and snatch the box out of his hands . . .
but I do nothing of the kind. I know the box
is empty – it must be – that he's finally lost
his mind, roused perhaps by a final urge
to extract some flare of magic from the clutter.

My foot falls on the gas and I inch away
slowly more dispirited than curious.
My children didn't seem to notice the box.
They would have wisecracked about it.
The rear-view mirror fogs with traces
of their innocence, of what's not seen.
But I'm looking backwards, of and off
course, and every direction seems identical,
as if where we go and what we see and do
are themselves the magic, the catastrophe.

LA BELLE DAME SANS MERCI

I met her at the designated hour of midnight
at the antiquated corner bar, The Napoleon House,
a place legend has it that supporters of the Emperor
planned to deposit after they rescued him from St. Helena's.
Well, now it's a hangout for artists, poets, musicians,
hangers on, even politicians like the egregious Ken Starr.
The Ramos Gin Fizzes are pretty bad, but if you sit
at a battered table in the back room you can control
the old phonograph and play whatever classical record
you crave. I sat up front because someone
had commandeered the music and indulged in a lot
of Poulenc, Dvorak and Eric Satie.
I wanted Bach and Shostakovich.

I arrived early of course, not because I rejoiced
at the idea of meeting a beautiful lesbian who planned
to chew me out for abandoning her friend, but because
I had nothing else to do. I ordered a succession
of vodka martinis and shot glasses of green chartreuse.
I piddled with napkins, wrote a few lines
in my journal, proceeded to get so drunk
that nothing anyone could say would phase me--
we're all dying, friend, start praying.
I knew I'd feel shitty the next day but, hell,
the next day was upon us, behind the curtain,
a twist of the doorknob, the lifting of a veil.

So she shows up, let's call her Sappho, I like that name,
I like the original's poetry—I burn, yeah, I burn too—
and she wears a slinky, tight fitting shift I think they call them,
garnet necklace and ear rings, patent leather shoes,
and, naturally, I brim with desire for the unattainable—
she has made a mission of denunciating men—
and she's here to dress me down for hurting her friend
who, by the way, is heterosexual.
She orders a glass of house Chablis because, she says,
it's cheap and she doesn't want to get drunk,
not tonight. "Can you go put on some Bach?"
she asks. No, I can't. Some dork controls the music.

So she gets right to the point, calls me despicable,
that her friend—let's call her Rafaela—
was really crazy about me and I just disappeared
after spending an afternoon with her when we lay
on the grass on the bank of one of the park lagoons,
I, reading Yeats to her, she listening, her hand
stroking my hip. "Why didn't you make love to her?"
Sappho demands to know. And on she went,
castigating me mercilessly, I the mouse to her cat.

I thought about defending myself, explaining that
Rafaela was so gorgeous and perfect, so supple
and kind that I felt terrified, that I feared plunging
into fathomless depths, that she surpassed me, a
Jaguar to my Ford Pinto, that I could not bear losing her
once I had succumbed . . . and, moreover, I could not read
her, had no idea she craved me, I saw only the cover
of that book, the pages seemed glued shut, you know,
that old game, the first-mover risks all, something like
god creating creation and wondering what went wrong—

But I said nothing, decided to appease Sappho,
the referee declaring a KO so she could spit in my face
and denounce me to the world as a low chauvinist
son-of-a-bitch once and for all—which perhaps I am.
And to think, your friend Alcaeus described you
as "violet-haired, honey-smiling Sappho."

In truth I was so zonked nothing mattered—call me a
hero, a coward, a narcissistic wretch, what's the difference?
Of a sudden the image of Rafaela on that bank, her pouty lips,
her dazzling eyes, her soothing flesh . . . I relived it all,
Sappho yapping away like some crazed insect,
I tossed Yeats into the lagoon, embraced her
and kissed her lips, yes, and she embraced me
and we thrived, a recollection of eternity in one
ambered second of the past, that vision, that redemption.
Which is why the past is superior to the present,
which is why the past justifies the future,
which is why time is the river you can always step into twice.

CAPITALISM

As I wait in the service lounge of Subaru, Inc.,
for an oil change and tire rotation, I wait among
dozens of others waiting, the communal tv changed
from the Supreme Court hearings to a home décor show,
I note the formidable majesty of this structure,
a capitalist arpeggio and crescendo, something
the Judge admires and will, when confirmed,
placate, make richer and absolve of any possible crimes
at the expense of us waiting here, we who have
little to begin with and will have less soon,
so that Ike's military-industrial complex will thrive
and metastasize forever under the extinct double eagle,
while we, even the workers here, tune into wallpaper
design, rich hues of latex, the latest in plastic siding
and ornamental doodads that we will charge
to Visa, Bank of America, to the invisible demigods
who pull switches at the top that make us dance
to their music, desire what they tell us to desire,
serve false consciousness disguised as sugar cookies,
which we take and eat, for this is their power,
kingdom and gaudy glory as it is
and has always been on earth because heaven
gets lost behind the charming façade of home décor.

GOLDFINCH

I had to put aside my re-reading
of Unamuno's *The Tragic Sense of Life*,
even the prose of which drips with tears,
because out of nowhere a flaming goldfinch
landed on the deck banister not two feet
from my patio chair, I had to sweep
Unamuno aside, I had to put the tragic
sense of life aside, I had to put myself
aside, given this golden omen,
this dazzling incarnation of light
before my eyes, its own eyes peering
into mine before it ascended
into the silver maple and melded
with its yellowing autumn leaves.
I had to put aside also this loss,
its suddenness as well, I had to put
my mind aside, I had to absorb the tree
and what the tree contained, though
hidden, I had to put aside belief--
and disbelief.

BRASS TACKS

Delve from the chromosome into
the molecules of nucleic acid, DNA,
delve further, probe nitrogen, hydrogen
and my favorite, sugar. It's us!
That component of sugar, ah,
I knew it, Honey, the sweetness
of your skin . . .
we're an assemblage of chemicals,
the whole, greater than its parts.
Delve still further, atoms . . . electrons,
neutrons, protons, then down again,
quarks. Where does it end?
What's inside a quark?
Color, spin, down, up and whatever.
Getting sort of abstract, don't you think?
Somehow, at bottom, we lose ourselves.
Somehow, at bottom, we become
everyone else.
Somehow, at bottom, the quanta
leap out from that vast gumbo
of nothingness.
Here we are, be proud, take my hand.

Louis Gallo

EMY'S PATIO, Bourbon Street

When the rat dropped
from the banana tree onto our table
we laughed and ordered more martinis.
Which the fiercer omen? That,
or the molten stare of the macaw
unruffled in its golden cage
by river breezes curling through
clacking tubes of bamboo
that rise like stirring rods
into the black soup of sky?

It's hot here. And wet.
I drink and seldom care
about bills, cancer and dirty air.
I peer into your sultry Aztec eyes
with tedious longing.
A blond Aztec?

Why was that rat perched
in our tree? Why do we eat
green pepper stuffed with peacock meat,
Oysters Margot and trout meuniere?
Will the world spin from our feet
or slink away in rodent fear
because we oblige old appetites?

You have spilled Tabasco on your blouse.
We laugh . . . as reality lolls
like a herd of cows.
We dance when we can, recite poems
and honk like quaint accordions.
I'll return alone some other night
to toast a ghostly summer moon
and crush the rat.

NARCISSUS

In Ovid's tale he pines over himself
in the mirrored water until he dies, but older versions
call it suicide. In either case it's Nemesis,
the spirit of retribution for hubris, who (that?) lures
him to the fatal pool. And, after all, what can we expect
from the son of a nymph and a river god?
Pausanias has the lad fall in love with his twin
sister rather than himself, and I assume
that's a tad healthier, though only a tad.

Seems like everybody gets off in some way
on the perversion: Freud's study: "On Narcissism,"
Narcissa Malfoy in Harry Potter, the emergency pod
in Alien, Russian ballet, Oscar Wilde, Gide . . .
But the real surprise is that earlier this morning
when we were both groggy and fogged with residual sleep
my wife pokes me in the ribs as I stand before the microwave
awaiting the ting and laughs, "I dreamed you left me
for another man, Pedro," (don't ask me why she calls me
Pedro). "Man?" I grunt, "Am I gay now?"

She pokes me again and I know all is well when so poked.
"It was a man all right, but it was you . . . a younger
version of yourself! You fell in love with your younger self."
And then she's off to the bath, I stuck with a rubbery
dish of eggs and hash browns, which I trash and opt
for a lousy Pop Tart. Plopping into the rocker
with a built-in Shiatsu massager, I lie back in wistful haze
as someone on CNN blasts Jodi Arias. My mind drifts
to the Egyptian pharaohs and their sister wives
and the old saw of women marrying men like their fathers
and vice versa. I rotate my neck and hear cartilage snap;

I'm stiff today; where is the energy of yesteryear?
My younger self? I imagine him at, say, twenty-five
or even thirty: lots of hair, boundless elan and libido,
ambition, passably good looking (though no Brad Pitt)
and with no doubt the arrogance of Faust . . .
I assure you, lest you scoff, I pay somber heed
to dreams (unlike the dreary Skinnerians who dismiss
them as neural short-circuits, so when it comes to dreams
I'm in league with David (or is it Daniel?) and Nebuchadnezzar.
I am flooded with sudden remorse. I want to have dreamed
that dream of falling in love with my youthful clone.
I demand the dream. I could go for it, whoever dreams it,

But as usual it's always the women on to us chumps
gazing at ourselves, our inner selves, our deepest yearnings–
which is why they stationed them in caves at Cumae,
which is why objects of ultimate desire must remain unknown,
which is why a Fall always cometh before Pride.

Louis Gallo

INFORMATION THEORY

She dips her long black soup spoon
into an earthen bowl of ratatouille
and sips for taste and believes
for that instant she has tasted God.
Any gain in information here
means an increase in entropy there.
At the moment of her rapture
Bolivia vanished into a sink hole.

The equations for information theory
and thermodynamic disorder are identical.
The more we learn, the faster
the universe disappears.
Think dark matter and energy.
Well, I'm no Shannon nor Szilard,
which should be obvious—
so I go by the popular glosses
and even then have a hard time
grasping the import.

But I know right now that my basement
is flooding and ice laminates
the front steps. Somebody somewhere
must be tasting God again.
And, oh, that ratatouille is platonic.
Be sure to cook the vegetables separately
before stirring them into the broth.
I prefer a lot of garlic and onions
but it's anybody's game.
My own information has dwindled
with the years. There must be
a new planet or star simmering
in the cosmic crockpot.

GUESTS

1
ARISTOTLE OVER FOR SUPPER

My beautiful young wife and I invited
Aristotle over for supper one night
because, frankly, no one thinks about him
much anymore and we felt he might be lonely.
He arrived with a cheap bottle of wine,
Sangria of all things, and looked disheveled
and downcast. He resented that line
by Wallace Stevens, "Aristotle is a skeleton"
(a line that has haunted me as well).
Who is not a skeleton? he asked not quite
rhetorically as he stroked my wife's blushed cheek.
"Your precious skin, my dear, is but a veneer,
a mask disguising the ghastly skull.   Terrible
to say, I know, but what can you do?"

I tried to change the subject to *The Poetics*.
I argued that tragedy befalls all of us
not merely the high and mighty, not
merely Oedipus or Hamlet because they
have regal blood. Aristotle shrugged,
"What difference does it make? If you
or your gorgeous wife [and here he stroked
her cheek again] die only a few people—

your friends, family—will know, remember
for a while then they too will die and
it will be as if you never existed. But
when Oedipus or Hamlet dies, we all remember.
That's the real difference—and precisely
because they have royal blood.
I asked about his former pupil Alexander.
"Ah, there's another. No one will forget him.
He was so arrogant and he never fully grasped
my Ethics. Conquered the entire known world
by his mid-twenties. His downfall, that is tragedy."

By this point I'd had it with the old lecher
trying to caress my wife and suggested he leave.
He understood, struggled to rise from the chair—
"arthritis, you know, the bones, the bones,
they survive despite it all"—
and slowly hobbled out of the door.
He hadn't eaten a bit of his blackened catfish
Linda had taken so much time to prepare.
A recipe straight out of Paul Proudhomme.
As I helped her wash the dishes, I noticed
a faint indentation on her cheek, a black
shadowy silhouette of five bony fingers.
I watched her lips hum softly as she
scraped away the catfish into our disposal.
For one horrific moment—it must have been
the angle at which sunlight filtered through
our muslin curtains—I thought I espied the bones
beneath her skin,

2
SOCRATES OVER FOR SUPPER

My beautiful young wife and I invited
Socrates for supper because we figured
he wouldn't try to fondle her
as did that old lech Aristotle
but also because I wanted to get something
off my chest that had been
giving me heartburn.
He arrived in his usual diaper, a most
unattractive site, with a bottle of ouzo.

My wife was busy preparing a great
Southern meal—grits, grillades,
fried catfish, shrimp remoulade . . .
The old man mumbled that he hated
everything except chicken
and I asked if he ever repaid that cock
to Asclepius.
He shook his head sadly. "It flew
the coop," he said and then I drank
the hemlock.

I do admire those who die for principle
but I wanted to know what he thought
about Nietzsche's idea that he had destroyed
the Western mind with that "know thyself"
business. I was surprised when he agreed.
"It was a mistake. Most of us should never
attempt to know ourselves. What we learn
may devastate our lives. Better to remain
animals."

But it's too late, I reminded him,
you changed the course and now
we have optimization of self, Dr. Phil,
Adler, Jung, Maslow, you know,
an entire industry that probes
the self, actualizes it, refines it,
corrects it, upgrades it—the self
has become something it's not.

Socrates swallowed a bite of the grits
and belched—"Hog food."
I went on about how I liked
the allegory of the cave but he stopped me—
"That's Plato, not I, and it's no allegory.
I was still mid-way between myth and reason
and Plato rationalized me, damn him."

As he prepared to leave, s smidgen
of grits still smeared on his lower lip,
he touched my wife on the cheek
with his stubby, yellowed finger:
"You are the Platonic form of beauty."
He turned to me and said, "Unknow
thyself, my friend. Stay in the cave."
He shook my hand and walked out
of the door, my wife blushing unabashedly.

3
FREUD OVER FOR SUPPER

I was a little worried about this guest
what with all those hysterical Victorian maidens
and the wretched, acrid cigars
but my beautiful young wife and I decided
to go ahead with the invitation
and she cooked up a sumptuous German meal—
sauerbraten, roulade, kasespatzle, rote grutze,
oh, she went all out . . .
he looked pretty haggard when he arrived
in his professorial tweeds beclouded
in cigar smoke.

I asked him about the pain in his jaw.
"Oh, it killed me," he said, "it always does."
I asked if he really believed that consciousness
was a disease.
"Of course it is, a deflection, a wrong turn
in evolution. It's obvious."
What about the meaning of life then,
you know, our purpose, our raison d'etre.
Freud shrugged, chuckled: "If you inquire
about the meaning of life you are sick."
He kept his eyes on my wife and eventually
took her dainty hand—
"Let me psychoanalyze you, my dear,
you remind me of Anna O."
She blushed and tried to slip her hand
out of his but he clutched her hard.

I tried to distract him, "Which
the greater force, Eros or Thanatos?"
We noticed he hadn't eaten a thing,
that the question alarmed him;
he puffed intently on his White Owl
and my wife and I could not stifle our coughs.
Eros and Thanatos, he growled,
are symbiotic, opposite sides of the same coin.
Eros thinks it can ward off the Beast
but it amounts to a mere ephemeral twitch.
He was on a roll:
"We lost paradise when we sublimated
polymorphous perversity into civilization
and its discontents. There's the expulsion
from the Garden, for you. We sit here
and discuss philosophy as we dine on this
fine food instead of making love,
which is what we really want to do."

He gazed directly into my wife's blue eyes
and I knew she felt his allure.
But you haven't touched the food, I said,
after all of her hard work.
"I must bid you adieu, I'm afraid. Jung
awaits me. I believe he plans a revolt.
So thank you for your hospitality and,
my dear, the offer still holds. I can cure you."
Soon he hobbled out of the door
and we dumped the food on his plate
into the disposal. It smelled like ashes.

Louis Gallo

THOREAU OVER FOR SUPPER

M pretty young wife asked
what she should fix for supper
when Thoreau came over and I told her
beans, he likes beans.
He arrived late, a bit disheveled
and said his jaw hurt, did we have
any ice? I recalled the sympathetic
symptoms of tetanus he experienced
when his brother died but didn't want
to bring it up. When he spoke
about solitude my wife and I glanced
at each other—no wonder he
didn't make it as an orator—
so harsh and high-pitched a voice.

I asked him what he thought about
Leon Edel's scathing essay
that debunked the whole Walden myth.
Thoreau shrugged, "Who's Leon Edel?"
He mumbled on, "I did set fire
to the woods and the villagers
denounced me but it was an accident—
I love trees more than people."
I asked him what he meant by
"quite desperation." He smiled,
gazed around at our apartment
and furnishings, which, admittedly,
we had bought on credit
and paid off little by little each month.

But you had a mirror in the cabin,
I blurted in self-defense! Why
would Thoreau need a mirror?
And your mother and sister brought
you food in picnic baskets every Sunday!
And sometimes the cabin was so packed
with visitors no one could move!
"That's Leon Edel speaking," he growled.
"I am eating canned beans here.
I hoed my own. They tasted so much
better. Sure, it was on Emerson's land
but so what? It was an experiment,
as I thoroughly (ha ha) explained."
Suddenly he had a coughing fit—
"I shouldn't have lain in the snow
to count those rings."
I'm afraid we saw a little blood
on his napkin, but at least he tried
to cover the hacking.

He reached over to touch my wife's cheek,
as all of our guests feel compelled to do,
and, of course, she blushed. It's not every
day that Thoreau touches your cheek.
He said he had to go—I think he only ate
one bean—because he'd lost a few things
he was trying to find. He bid us adieu
from the doorway, blew kisses, and whispered
"Moose."

Louis Gallo

D.H. HOLMES DEPARTMENT STORE CLOCK

Every Monday noon my grandfather
begrudgingly cranked up his golden Chrysler Imperial
to drive his wife and her three sisters to Canal Street
where he dropped them off at the D.H. Holmes clock,
the ultimate meeting place of the city.
Begrudgingly because he hated the sisters and they
hated him because he was an arrogant bastard
who looked down upon them for marrying bums.
I loved him because he was an arrogant bastard
who put up with no crap from anyone.
I loved the sisters because they were sweet, humble
and kind. I loved my grandmother because
she was the only person in this universe
who stood up to him and usually got her way.
Three almost identical old ladies dressed
in identical navy blue outfits. There was something
formal and decorous about it, unlike today
when decorum has reduced to "Have a Good Day'
from McDonald's or Burger King.
This was before malls and cell phones
so once Grandfather dropped them off
they went incommunicado as they swept through
all four or five floors of Holmes then proceeded
to the rival Maison Blanche in the next block.
They might even wander down to Woolworth
if they had time. But never to the other side

of Canal which had already become seedy
with its naked girl theaters and dubious magic shops.
My grandfather picked them up at five
and that was that. I remember the stockings
and identical navy purses, sometimes the navy
hats with veils. I remember the lavish austerity,
the hint that something elegant was about to disappear.
Three models to choose from then—Chrysler,
Chevrolet and Ford. And Grandfather always
chose those Imperials which he liked better than Cadillacs.
This long before the Balkanization of Bell Telephone,
before franchised chains annihilated private businesses.
Grandfather would drive to Southern Radio on Tulane
to chat with Alphonse, the owner, after he deposited
those ladies under the clock; then he made some rounds
until he picked them up at five. The sisters
never stopped talking; it was chatter, chatter, chatter,
and laughter, they laughed a lot, though three of them
were practically indigent. None had gone to college.
None aspired to more than they had, though what they had
wasn't much aside from each other. Decorous, even noble,
stalwart—and, this is true, enviable.

Louis Gallo

THE STREETS OF THE VIEUX CARRE
(perpendicular to Canal)

Decatur

The seedy one, way down near the U.S. Mint,
grunge, decay, drunks, leather bars,
junk shops, rancid dives--
my favorite part, where I used to work
for that underground newspaper,
. . . yet up beyond Central Grocery
gets touristy, beignets at Café du Monde,
Iowans clutching Hurricanes, gift shops,
the old Jax Brewing Company spewing hops
through the air as the calliopes rang out
You Are My Sunshine, until they converted it
into a multi-level shopping mall,
and, ah, across the street Las Casas de los Marinos,
one of the then roughest bars, three or four rooms
of it, fistfights all the time, crowded
like Mardi Gras, all the time,
the juke playing La Bamba,
where I caroused, where someone punched
me in the face

Chartres

Mostly quiet and sleepy, but . . .
The Napoleon House
where I hung out a lot, altered mindstates,
and swilled yellow chartreuse
while listening to Ravel and Prokofiev—
ah, the times there, privileged moments,
the sadness and joys, the very bad
Ramos Gin Fizzes,
Ken Starr and Newt Gingrich, enemies,
where my great grandfather lived
during the yellow fever epidemic
and survived to write a famous march,
The French Market Buzzards

Royal

Fine antiques, art galleries, where
the uppity and would-be uppity go
to stroll and spend,
formal, ritzy gift shops,
not t-shirts and Mardi Gras beads—
look, a fake marble Venus de Milo,
ten-feet high gazing from a storefront window,
a street I love but avoid,
too high class, snotty,
back yard of the Cathedral
where under mercury vapor splash
we watched Comus drift by—
and it's where you catch to NOPSI bus
near Canal, outside Woolwowrth,
out to Gentilly

Burgundy

Pronounce it BurGUNdy.
Mostly shadows, domestic, quiet,
but once a raucous bar called Déjà vu
and a fabulous candlelit restaurant,
The Burgundy House, run by transvestites
where she and I mooned and drank
vodka martinis, preparing for the night—
      best poppy seed dressing
      we'd ever tasted,
      (to this day)
our waiter, tall, silent wearing
neon pink hot pants and a halter,
his/her hair a platinum cloud
that emitted light
by which we gazed into each other's eyes

Dauphine

I lived for a year at the cross street
of Ursulines, a two-story stucco building
with a wrought-iron grill work balcony
from which you could see a speck of Canal Street—
every day I walked the entire Quarter
from this nexus, the gay neighbor
across the street sunning on his balcony
wearing only a jock strap—
my landlady, nosy, rapping on my door
the minute she spotted a fruit fly,
legendary Jim Garrison three doors
down toward the river—
the banes: roars of busses hurtling
toward Canal, street cleaner shovels
scraping the asphalt at seven a.m.—
try sleeping through that.
Nothing much else on Dauphine,
houses built during the Spanish occupation
of Alexjandro O'Reilly, few pedestrians,
though every now and then someone
totally naked in a full indian headdress

Louis Gallo

Rampart

Nobody goes there—a main artery,
four lanes I think—ugly, semi-industrial,
one edge of the Quarter,
aside from the International Shrine of St. Jude
for the Hopeless
across the street from a crumbling
brick wall about twelve-feet high,
maybe a nunnery—
when hopeless I visited that shrine
never getting past the vestibule
where they tack gold replicas
of human organs on wall-sized
bulletin boards, thousands of mini-
organs all squashed together,
tokens of the limitless hopeless—
ah, but up the street, where
it becomes the old Basin Street,
near Canal and one of the venerable
cemeteries,
a dozen or so wild lesbian bars,
most vibrant in town, where
I, who cannot dance,
danced the night away
with women so beautiful
you wished you were one yourself

NEVER START OR END A STORY WITH A DREAM

. . . yeah, a dream all right, or was, few nights ago, the best dream of my life because when so cocooned I felt the serenity of timelessness, love, beauty, all that and more . . . so let me record it now before, as all dreams, it dissolves:

I step into a New Orleans café full of art deco prints on the walls. It resembles the old Marti's Restaurant on Rampart except Marti's has shifted on its axis and is now horizontal to Canal Street up yonder . . . and everything behind Marti's is chaos, evil, scary, dark, whereas all affronting it – light and bustle, the usual Quarter.

well, I step in and scout for a booth and find one in the middle of the aisle, so I slide over to the window draped with bamboo shades, and soon a middle-aged waitress appears, her wrinkles and eroded face alarming, and I tell her I'm waiting for someone and can't order yet. She huffs away as you approach from behind and slide softly beside me and I'm overjoyed to see you and smile a big one and you lean against my shoulder, and we hook into each other's eyes and can't stop smiling...

"Hey You," I grin, and you reply, "Hey you," and grin, and we're smiling like idiots, lips stretched to our temples in gladness, and I say again, "Hey you," and you too, "Hey you," and we're pressed together, you in a green floral shirt and those wondrous tight jeans I love and afflicts all other girls with pangs of jealousy. I wrap my arm around you, and grin again "Hey you," and we sort of forget we were to meet and head out for the airport for a flight to Manhattan.

We just linger, embracing, and I smell the essence of you, the scent of ambrosia, of youth, and I inhale you, inhale and reel with delight and thanksgiving, for in this dream I am about twenty-eight, and you, twenty-two, and we're young and unencumbered and mad over each other, and nothing else matters, the way I like it, nothing to matter, and time obliterates itself, and I lick your cheek and taste you, and feel the warmth of your arms and shoulders and there is nothing, no amount of money, no act of Congress to save the planet, no cure for cancer, there is nothing I would trade for this moment for, a moment the dream magic makes eternal, and "Hey You," I laugh again, and you, "Hey You too" . . .

and then it ended, how a door slams shut, and I lay flat on the bed, my face smashed into the mattress, feeing horrible and desolate – and understood that real doors can never be reopened.

LEGS

When they cut off my Uncle Henry's legs I was off smoking weed with a girl who said she was the great-great-great niece of President William Henry Harrison, the one who never made it to the White House. I remember an efficiency rank with cat piss and stale Purina, a green cotton spread on the mattress, Southern Comfort, vanilla candles, and Jim Morrison in the background, her favorite, though I inclined toward Jackie Wilson or Ben E. King. I'd hate to think we reached the sublime right as that blade dug into my uncle's bones which must have smelled grisly like when dentists drill into some sick molar.

He was a big man who would capture you at reunions and boom the secrets of direct marketing, mail order and free advertising into your face. My cousins and I tried not to meet his eye, but he always cornered Sandy because at the time she had those new breasts which he always managed to brush against. Back then it disgusted us, though now I think I understand; I was out trying to do the same thing, not with Sandy, although she too crossed my mind. He just seemed so old and his teeth had turned into kernels of corn. He had a wife, of course, my mother's sister, but aunts and mothers don't figure when it comes to love you can call love.

The decline began when a drunk broadsided Uncle's van and they had to pry him out with crowbars and two-by fours. A miracle he survived, everybody said. Broken ribs, two crushed legs, spleen damage. There's more, always more, but at some point you lose count. We saw him a few times buzzing around in a wheelchair with two massive casts on his legs. The doctors discovered diabetes during their probe and that's what finally ruined him, not the accident. His skin started to swell and blacken. Gangrene. Long after the broken bones had mended.

Years later I saw him out at his ranch-style house in Picayune, where my family and I drove for a mercy visit -- even I dimly aware that a finale had commenced. He slumped in the same wheelchair with a green shawl hiding the missing legs. He didn't talk much anymore but sometimes he'd laugh at a joke or groan. Aunt Ruth said he had high fever all the time and felt horrible. He no longer tried to corner anybody and his voice had shriveled to distant static. He didn't even notice Sandy, who'd come along for the ride. I saw him pick at a tray of cheese cubes stabbed with party toothpicks. Mostly, he sat in the corner and stared at some game show on television.

Before the funeral I had too much to drink. My sister, cousins and I clumped together in a vestibule. I'd brought along a new girlfriend who smirked a lot as we made snotty comments about relatives we hated. Everyone wore black except us who planned to invade the French Quarter soon as we could slip away from the wake. My mother had dragged me over to the casket to take a last look at the man who once spent an entire day locating a suitcase of mine; the railroad has lost it on my trip to New Jersey, where Uncle and his family lived before he retired back home to the south. It was easy and free staying with them while I spent my days and most of the nights prowling Manhattan. I never thanked my uncle for his trouble.

We headed straight for Bourbon Street. My cousins and sister disappeared soon enough and I wound up in Lafitte's Blacksmith shop with Wanda, who smoked two cigarettes at once, white fangs dangling from the meat of her glossy violet lip. I drank vodka martinis until all the shitty things she said about life, love, politics, men and God shrank into the screech of some pitiful insect. But, God, she had gorgeous legs, chiseled, they seemed, right out of a vat of Coppertone.

Someone started to plunk "I'm Walking" on the bar piano and patrons gathered round to sing. Dimly, I heard Wanda call my uncle a pig. It was my fault. I'd told her all the stories. But just then I felt pretty sorry for him. "You don't know one God-damned thing," I growled as the room spun. When I stood up to leave my knees quivered and I knew I was headed straight down before I got anywhere, faster than that dumb president who missed the White House or an old man with no legs.

CROW

Crow squats upon a rail
some twenty feet above the parking lot
where, between classes, students
come and go, some waiting at the bus stop,
others passing from building
to building.
I am on the same level as Crow
but behind him (her?) near the magnolia.
Crow knows I am here and cocks
his head every so often to check
if I'm still safely distant.
He starts to squawk, an itinerant preacher
haranguing the crowds below
delivering, I assume, dire messages
about perilous futures and coming plagues,
the need to repent or at least
slow down.
No one stops to listen or pay attention
to a wise, cacophonous black bird
who speaks with a different tongue.
Isaiah on the mountain.

CLEANING LADY

When the cleaning lady, Dora, comes in
to empty the trash and sometimes dust
the desks and bookshelves (her schedule
and my office hours must be identical)
she's usually huffing and pushing
a massive apparatus of dusters, paper
towels, fluids and waste bins,
and when it's Friday, she cracks
a crooked smile and rejoices,
"Thank God, it's Friday," and I rejoice
with her.   Our rapport is limited—grunts
about the weather, the poorly constructed
building, her grandkids, my daughters,
the usual chit-chat with those you really
know nothing about, nor they you . . .
but friendly enough. And I think she senses
a certain camaraderie between us, and, if so,
she's right. I often envy her, simple, easy
work . . . unlocking doors, dumping trash,
feathering the shelves—no torturous thought
to it however physically arduous. (I would
prefer the night shift, however, when
nobody else is around.)

I never talk to Dora about what I'm brooding
over—the introjection of false consciousness
into the mass mindset, the statute of limitations
riveted in all of us at birth, the sublime
in the pedestrian, the travesty of minimum
wage (as if anyone . . .), the phenomenology
of desire, Hegel's absurd dialectics . . .
how on and on it goes. Perhaps she too
so broods and doesn't share with me,
but I doubt it. Dora seems salt of the earth,
get the job done, go home, drink some beer,
watch a latest episode.

She's not young either, though younger than I—
who isn't? She too has a bad lower back.
She too needs more money, more pleasure,
more everything. But she seems content enough,
never miserable, never hostile, never complaining.
Whereas I . . . I do envy her, wish her the best,
hope they give her a raise, that her grandkids
cherish her. I know each new day that I will
enter a clean, dust-free office as once again
I wrestle the black angels of false consciousness

ALL I WANNA IS NORMAL!

Of course, son, as we all know nothing's normal.
Well, maybe that unsalted soda cracker
with no pimento cheese spread, no jalapeno,
no nothing but bland wafer that, I swear
reminds me of the Eucharist. No normal
but plenty of bland like those who smile sweetly—
not the good sweet but that habitual trademark,
a sign of hope they won't be further crushed,
who watch Vanna White spin Fortuna's wheel,
who dream of bank accounts . . .
the subterfuge is giant, could be veneer,
below which seethe dragons.
The universe ain't normal.
But you, boy, with all your darkness,
foreboding rising from your skull like smoke,
your whole body a tattoo, Bosch's hell,
your outrage, venom, *not if but when*,
your life, debris, shrapnel . . .
you, get some Nabisco quick,
gobble down those baked tidbits
like crazy til you dissolve some.
Then you're on your way.
Not normal, never you, but maybe
a ball room dance or two, or waltz,
that you can enjoy. But watch the tangos!

ER

Three nights ago my wife and I
Spent hours in the emergency room
Tending our severely allergic child
Who had by error consumed . . . millk . . .

Milk, the Everyfood, manna,
Whole, complete, protein dew,
But selfsame stuff poison to
Our fragile, tender daughter.

And many others since as I've read
Lactose tolerance is a mutation
From way back, when no one
Could digest the stuff.

Not so much the turbulence
Of that flaming systemic rash
Nor her terror-stricken eyes
And now, I pause, to think upon

Such maelstrom, not so much the milk
Of evil or that she might have died --
I think instead of nothing, nothing
As if stricken in the brain

With knowledge dread enough to crush
Thought flat, curdling in the drain.

WITTGENSTEIN: A BIOGRAPHY

The young man detested their silly giggling in the cafes.
Bright ribbons fluttered in the usual girls' hair.
Psychoanalysts passed in silken, black carriages.
Assassination and hemophilia troubled the empire.
A new theory of light drove him into cold, dim rooms.
He stood on a corner in Vienna and felt inches shorter.
A horse snorted. The new century severed time like an ax.
"Reality begets language!" he cried to no one.

The same reality betrayed him. He never smiled,
stroked a severe violin as his brothers killed themselves.
His youthful decorum hardened into zeal
and he listened for breathing beneath the ink.
He imagined words so refined they split throats
until safer, more prudent words floated
through his mind like balloons. He was wrong.
There was only language.
He stopped talking and disappeared for years.

He returns to sulk on the patios of wry philologists.
The infinite but unbounded universe had expanded.
War hero, school master, common gardener,
he entertained the philological wives:
"Philosophy," he teased, "is a battle against
the bewitchment of an intelligence by means of language."
He accompanied students to Walt Disney movies
in a personal dome of gloom, insisting his aim
was "to show the fly the way out of the fly bottle."
On the day he died he shot up in bed, wild-eyed,
beseeched his last disciple, "Tell them I've lived
a wonderful life!"

SECRETS

You wouldn't want these old secrets,
dulled by their own patina of sorrow and deceit,
unearthed by prim young technicians who employ
not divining rod nor hunch nor pure love,
like mad Schliemann hungering toward the tomb
of Priam, but the cool precision of gauges
and instruments which can extract voltage from pain:
you want them excavated by craven fool, traitor,
whiskey priest, whore and whore-monger, fallen angel,
trustees of whatever quivers in midnight sweats--
the slit wrist, empty bottles of booze and pills,
gas leaking from unlit ovens--
you want a custodian of secrets like yourself,
knowing in your blood that instruments
tell far greater and more beautiful lies,
measure only what can be measured,
will never glimpse the real Jerusalem
where flowers bloom when gazed upon
and you breathe not air but cream
and no amount of money or pleasure
can ever change your mind.

Louis Gallo

THE QUEEN IS DEAD, LONG LIVE THE QUEEN

When the four of us once walked our dogs
up and down the rolling hills, through meandering streets,
sometimes by the river, sometimes the wilderness
of Wildwood, it was always Daisy first stampdeing
the way, tugging us, often knocking us off our feet,
and the younger Peaches, heeding the Alpha female,
her best friend . . .
                        until that day Daisy lagged behind,
older now, and I caught Peaches catching Daisy's eye,
I caught the moment Daisy abdicated, and I caught
Peaches trot in front of her, Daisy now following,
no longer exploding with energy, no longer Alpha
and so relieved that Peaches now assumed the power,
and dragged us along Peaches did with all her might,
but never, never with the might of Daisy, Daisy
now trailing behind with us, Peaches, panting,
leading the charge.

"A LOOSELY CONSTRUCTED THING"

Thus, William James, defining the self . . .
hinting that we consist of mere disguises
of ourselves, what with the battered luggage
of the past, that mandolin, saxophone, and flute,
pounding international Morse code on a
brass telegraphic key, the old library at Lee Circle
with its Alexandria of musty, dusty books—
our pasts, perhaps the collective pasts
of others as well, and why not? Carthage,
Nineveh, Shiloh, Weimar, the ant mound
of interconnections, and not only the past,
but the present, less the omega Now
but rather a sort of sprawl, yesterday, the day
before, tonight, tomorrow, next week,
a kind of omelet of smeared time . . .
and of course the future, that diffusion,
way beyond next week or month, which
we still calculate as Now (check out date
books), how we imagine ourselves when
transfigured, basking in Oahu, promoted
to vice-suzerain of the neo-Ottoman Empire,
retired and hale, worth a fortune—
tightly constructed, the bedazzled self,
mesmerized by mirrors, look Ma *cette moi!*
costumes, veneer, can't put your finger
on it though we sign on the dotted lines,

Louis Gallo

collect passports and licenses and Visas
to preserve the illusion of continuity
while the true self may be hoisted between
two cactuses on a desert hammock north
of Santa Fe in 1961 listening to NBC News
reporting on an invasion of the Bay of Pigs--
a transistor radio, a bottle of mescal,
dreaming about the atomic bomb.

Acknowledgments

"Crash," *Litro*
"Zero/Infinity," *Xavier Review*
"Mother Opens the Family Album," *Convergence*
"Irony," *Tampa Review*
"Burning," *Poetrymagazine*
"The Undertaker's Daughter," *Mississippi Review*
"University Pool," *Poetry Midwest*
"Jonathan Edwards," "Socrates Over for Supper," "Freud Over for Supper," "Thoreau Over for Supper," "Narcissus," "Wittgenstein," *Pennsylvania Literary Journal*
"Black Box," *Houston Literary Review*
"Bugsy," *Thema*
"Legs," *bio-Stories*
"Never Start or End a Story with a Dream," *Mash Stories*
"Aristotle Over for Supper," *A-Minor Magazine*
"Emy's Patio," *Arlington Literary Journal*
"Dream Recipe," *Eclectic Flash*

About the Author

Louis Gallo is the founding editor of the now-defunct journals, *The Barataria Review and Books: A New Orleans Review*. His work has been nominated for the Pushcart Prize several times. He is the recipient of a NEA grant for fiction. He teaches at Radford University in Radford, Virginia.

www.ingramcontent.com/pod-product-compliance
Lightning Source LLC
Chambersburg PA
CBHW032236080426
42735CB00008B/880